Inspired Perspectives

*For information regarding Cornelia J. Krikke, email her at
info@transformative-practices.com
Sign up for her newsletter at transformative-practices.com*

Praise For Inspired Perspectives

I loved this book. I read it in one sitting. Cornelia's words moved me into a deeply embodied state, full of hums and aches and thrums. Her writing evoked memories of childhood play in the forest, loved ones lost and found, as well as moments of unspeakable bliss. Her work is both elegiac and celebratory, like a prayer to the complex experience of being human.— **Dani Vedros, LCSW Director, Studio of the Healing Arts, Psychologist, Author, Speaker**

When I settled into this book, I saw that what I was reading was a collection of love stories; including the profound love Cornelia and Gary shared, the subsequent loss and pain, and the inevitable renewal of the human soul. Cornelia's message is simple: we have no choice but to choose life. The tales she tells highlight how through love we can reclaim ourselves by observation and reflection. What are some of the keys? Simple connection, awareness of our daily lives, respect for intimacy and gratitude for magical moments. We make choices to notice our connections. Cornelia reminds us to choose well! — **Dr. Jack Muskat, Psychologist, Author, Speaker**

This lovely book inspires us to purposefully create our own lives, but with empathy and compassion for others. The book documents stories and poems of individual transformation but the teachings are universal, for every reader will recognize experiences we share with those who have contributed their journeys. Through the author's insightful and loving work, we are brought closer together and also closer to Nature and to Source. Guided to break through (and from) old, sabotaging patterns, we shift our perspectives, open to Grace and touch the numinous. This book's arrival is timely – to help us through personal and global troubled times.— **Marilyn Walker, Ph.D & Professor Emeritus, Author, Artist, Shamanic Practitioner**

Nourishment for the soul; these stories pique the senses through a unique, direct style of storytelling. It is guaranteed that these vignettes and poems will stay in your thoughts long after they are read. There is real magic in this book.— **Christina A. Cavanagh, Author, Managing your E-mail: Thinking Outside the Inbox**

Tender, poignant, at turns poetic, Cornelia Krikke's prose inspires like a fresh breeze.— **Lisa Lipsett, Ph.D, Author, Beauty Muse**

Cornelia and I share the same island with awe-inspiring mountains and vast ocean energy. *Inspired Perspectives* successfully helped me reignite my own personal inner vision and have a greater appreciation and more gratitude for the beauty we all share. After reading the vignettes, I saw trees, water and wildlife with new eyes and felt them through multiple senses. Her invitation to explore our lives with an active imagination has birthed vivid insights about our mutual dance, with nature and with each other. Read *Inspired Perspectives* and savor the rainbow of inner visions that blossom.— **Allen M. Schoen, MS, DVM, Ph.D, Author of Kindred Spirits, How the Remarkable Bond Between Humans and Animals Can Change the Way We Live**

In my life and in my work as a Chief Psychologist at Toronto District School Board, I have learned that the unexpected often happens. My PhD was on Learned Helplessness, where we became unable to move or change because we THINK we can't change anything, even when a simple solution is right by us. To cope, and even more, to fully live, we must be able to grow and change. Cornelia has given us a path and guidance for change. There are miracles even when the path is dark and this book

teaches us about them. The short story aspect of the book is refreshing and the parts about deep love are especially moving.
— **Ruth Baumal, Ph.D,**

Insights have the energy required to rearrange existing structures. Stagnant edifices can be internal and external.

Bringing the lens of imaginative brilliance to our assumptions carries us over internal prison walls and delivers us to broader understanding.

Play with imagination as a means of loosening outdated thought.

Cultivate habits.

Engineer a path to greater experience of joy and wisdom.

Be daring.

Dedication

For my husband, Gary B. Allison

March 14, 1948 to April 23, 2015

Thank you for the love, the play, the lessons, the healing.

Acknowledgments

I am grateful to all who have inspired, cajoled, and challenged me. We stand on the shoulders of those before us. Our potential is mulched, enriched, and pollinated by others.

I thank Gary, my late husband, for always seeing the good and possible. Gary invariably inspired me to stretch with creative flow. He emboldened me and buoyed me. Gary's constancy facilitated releasing the need to understand. I thank him for applauding me while he was alive and for the continuing encouragement I feel.

Several of the vignettes are drawn from the lived experience of those I know. Other stories are not told here, but do inform this work. I am profoundly indebted to those who have shared intimate, vulnerable conversations with me. Sharing the inner world of another is one of the greatest experiences I know. To be trusted enough for another to stand naked with us is powerful intimacy. These are tender exchanges.

Thank you to the many individuals who have inspired me to flower uniquely. In a world of normative pressure, those who walk their own path have heartened me to express and birth the particular seeds latent within.

The encouragement of friends first came at a book club evening. We each brought some of our own writing to share. The talent in the room was staggering. I read my prose to praise; praise that instilled the confidence to begin this book.

Darlene Nielsen has supported this project and deserves special mention. Thank you also to my early readers; Jo Bateman, Lesley Spinks, Samantha Parker, Taylor & Louise Devlin, and Brian Allison.

Importantly, I bow to spirit, source energy, the creative vastness from which we appear to emerge, and from which we are inseparable. Flowing with original energy heals us and inspires us. I hope words in this book bring you deeper appreciation of your own beautiful abundance.

Table of Contents

Foreword

Reading this book is an experience like no other. Here in your hand is a beautiful seamless blend of living poetry and prose—one that succeeds gloriously in its goal of reminding us that a taste of freedom and grace is ours—if only we are willing to shift out of our rigidly held mindset and habitual points of view.

Cornelia Krikke reminds us that we are all caught in a polarized world of opposites viewing life as requiring a constant need to make judgments about good and bad, right and wrong. Through this lens of judgment, we so often see ourselves as embattled and in opposition to this world--separate, different and in many ways threatened by all around us that is not "me". We live estranged in some degree not only from others but from Nature herself. Yet we are in our essence Nature and it is our sacred task and responsibility not to judge, but to welcome as She does, all that is.

Toward this end Cornelia offers us the practice of Active Imagination, showing us through beautiful poetic imagery and profound tales of transformation, how to step out of our tension-filled world of opposites, and to embody and see through the eyes of the "other".

I am reminded in Cornelia's beautiful prose of what the poet Rainer Maria Rilke once spoke in a "Letter to a Young Poet": "Perhaps everything that frightens us is, in its deepest essence, something helpless that wants our love. ...Seek out some simple and true feeling of what you have in common with (others) ...when you see them, love life in a form that is not your own..."

Of course, it is not always simple to release our prized perspective and to see life through others' eyes. Change rarely comes in a flash and we are often called to hold the tension and endure until a new perspective emerges that is more in alignment with the wholehearted compassionate energy of life. Yet, Cornelia assures us that "Genesis happens through each of us" and that there is always a new creative solution to every puzzle. But we must be co-creators with life and she implores us to accept responsibility for our intentions and choices.

I hope that you will find, as I did, how *Inspired Perspectives* reads like a prayer that magically transforms the seeming ordinariness of experience, bringing a visceral energy, warmth and color to the often washed out palette of our daily life. - **David Gordon, Author, Mindful Dreaming, A Practical Guide for Emotional Healing Through Transformative Mythic Journeys**

Introduction

Inspired Perspectives is a collection of prose and poetry exploring impressions in an often playful, manner. I invite you to enjoy a journey through these pages. Likewise, I encourage you to see everyday events with playful panoramic vision.

When we choose to genuinely embody and to understand an alternative perspective, we have a new lens. Think of the many facets of a gem. Each facet is unique and reflects the light before it. Or recall the often told story, of several blindfolded people who are standing around an elephant; each person is touching a different part of the elephant. Participants try to describe the animal to each other; long tube of a trunk, stump of a leg, vastness of a belly. Differing perspectives, without an overall understanding, cause the participants to believe they are describing something unrelated. This is often true for each of us, as we try to describe our understanding and experience.

Knowing our own hidden, often under acknowledged, dominant perspectives, gives us power. Viewing from alternative perspectives helps us to see our habitual thought patterns. The ability to broaden our vision enables us to see situations more clearly, recognize opportunities, and better understand the others in our lives.

Some of the prose in this book is partly imaginative. The *Lilacs* vignette presents thoughts and memories of a woman accompanied by the feelings of the lilac bush she sits beneath. These examples allow us to stretch our imagination beyond the normal treadmill of thought and encourage alternate perspectives to emerge. Many of the stories you will read describe the experience people had in daily life; experiences of pivoting their view and arriving at deeper understanding. Several stories recount grace filled moments, reflecting what each of us yearns for and occasionally tastes. These stories inform at a fundamental level and they are the treasures held close to our hearts.

After you have read *Inspired Perspectives* once, you may choose to return and dip into a section randomly. The format transitions from chapter one, *Prelude*, to *Stirring Perception,* through *Shifting Perspectives,* and finally to *The Numinous.*

Prelude reminds us that we are creative beings; engaging in creation, whether we are aware or not, in each moment of our lives. Accepting responsibility for this inevitable partnering is a life's opportunity and work. Moment to moment our thoughts and feelings have impact. Our intentions and choices matter; always shifting our lives and the lives of those around us in subtle and profound ways.

Stirring Perception illustrates how active imagination, 'what ifs', teach us to expand our mental and emotional landscape. This practice is akin to the physical practices we might engage in at the gym as we increase our capacity. Active imagination helps us to build the facility to understand multiple perspectives, and it can also reward us with delightful moments of whimsy and joy.

Shifting Perspective includes stories where an alternative perspective changed someone's way of relating. Softening the edges of our beliefs and our defenses is a tall request. When challenged, each of us has a set of reflexive responses. Likewise, each of us tends to bolster our offensive position or retreat perhaps with passive aggressive sabotage. The stories in this chapter are moments of breakthrough to new ways of relating, leading to more authentic outcomes for all of the participants.

Numinous Experience is a collection of stories expressing important and potent moments. I am profoundly grateful to the people who trusted me with these precious gems.

The final chapter, *Afterword,* I give suggestions on ways to engage in perspective shifts.

~~~

Notice the next time you feel inspired. Notice how bright you feel. Notice how a broadened perspective gives you access to emotional, mental, and physical resilience. This may at times open us to understanding something we'd rather not understand or have in our life. Yet underneath, there is a strength to deal with whatever has emerged.

Enjoy your experience as you read *Inspired Perspectives*. Play with active imagination, be curious, ask questions.

A note on the use of first person

The vignettes are told in the first person whether they are my story, a bird's tale, or the story of another.

A note on the poetry in this book

Some of the sections are written in a style closer to poetry. This was not my intention. Rather, this is just the way the words arrived when I shifted my attention to the topics.
~~~

Section 1. Prelude

We are creative beings with the agency to expand our individual perspectives. We can contribute to positive shifts in our communities. At essence, we are inseparable from perpetual creative energy. The world is not divided between creatives and non-creatives. We are all creative.

How we use our imagination, insight, and generative skills, is another matter. Do we develop control over our attention in such a way that we can stay with the brilliance we have accessed? Can we recognize moments of essential understanding? Do we act on insights? Our creativity is multidimensional. It happens as often in the boardroom as at the easel.

As I work with clients in business, consulting, and coaching, I am continually delighted to witness imaginative solutions, breakthroughs, and radically new ideas. As I watch new solutions enacted, I see the changing of an old paradigm of frustration to a new experience of ease.

When we extend our realm of question, perspective, imagination, we cultivate new possibility. The resources we each have access to, are by definition, much greater than our current understanding. The world is continually birthing and shifting. Genesis happens through each of us. Our task is one of aligning and attending.

Individually and collectively we hold the key to the mysteries before us. Let us not be diminished by a current challenge; rather view the puzzle as evidence there is a creative solution available. Our task then is to weave a personal and collective pathway forward.

Wise scholars and poets describe the ground of being, where individual and collective understanding is always emerging.

Mary Oliver and Jalāl ad-Dīn Muhammad Rūmī are two of my favorites. I encourage you to claim the mythic realm as your own. Recognize that we share a field much greater than our intellectual and philosophic lens. New understanding is continually coming forth, like a perpetual stream.

Insights and new perspectives have the energy required to rearrange existing structures. Stagnant edifices can be internal and external. Bringing the lens of imaginative brilliance to our assumptions, carries us over internal prison walls and delivers us to broader understanding. Play with imagination as a means of loosening outdated thought. This loosening may open to mysterious, awe inspiring moments. We touch the numinous.

Holding The Tension of Opposites

One of the obstacles to change is polarized attitudes, that is movement toward opposing viewpoints. Polarization tends to happen. In politics, sports, business and personal relationships, we easily see how the drift toward opposing polar views takes place. Likewise within our own mind, emotions, and habits, we have polarity. For example, our partner likely has qualities that we both admire and judge. For an inner example, we may believe strongly in protecting the environment yet be a poor model for recycling.

Eastern traditions light up the tendency towards polarity, describing yin and yang. Yin energy continues and eventually reverses to yang. Yang energy expands, eventually reversing to yin. The middle path is often exalted and is often misunderstood. The middle path need not be mediocrity. Rather the middle path that is proposed, is a choice to incorporate an understanding of polarity, and an understanding of holding the tension of opposites.

Carl Jung and others have discussed holding the tension of opposites as a means to facilitate a totally new, previously unimagined, third path. The third path they speak of is an innovative solution elevated above the current viewpoint and previous vision. The challenge for each of us is to hold our attention steady, and our judgement at bay, during trying times. We must become comfortable with uncertainty and comfortable resisting an easy either-or solution to the decisions that press us. Like pregnant mothers, we patiently attend to our wellbeing as a fresh living viewpoint emerges. During the gestation period, uncertainty is inevitable. To bring the new into objective reality, this time of invisibility is necessary. This is creative action.

In a troubled, divisive world, refraining from judgment, refraining from absolute-ism, and refraining from being too sure of ourselves, facilitates miracles of understanding, scientific breakthroughs and regenerative moments. This too is creative action.

Actively looking at opposites facilitates expansion. What is there that is good in an opposing viewpoint? What is good about this challenge? What is disturbing about this opportunity? One means we use to answer our calling, is exploring the garden of our thoughts. What do I assume to be true? What else, seemingly different, might also be equally true? Might I be completely wrong and the opposing view, completely right? Am I curious? Can I develop and hold a sense of identity that is positive and independent of the need to be 'right' or to 'understand'? When we trust and relax, the answer will come. This is creative action.

We Live As Part Of A Nurturing Planet

We live as part of a beautiful planet and are not separate from any aspect of her. We are rooted in nature. We are nature; cells, electrical charges, tissue which separates to water, mineral and gas. What we call life, perpetual dynamic force animating our form, also animates the form of animals and plants around us. Old religions attribute unbridled mythic power to nature gods. We evolved as a species bowing in wonder, reverence, and awe to gigantic mystery. We evolved celebrating, sacrificing, and seeking communion.

Modern city life distances us from our indisputable, interwoven connection with all of life. In our center we innately respond with a smile and joy when witnessing a spring flower. As we lay on the ground by an ancient tree awe may flood us. When we wade in the ocean on a warm day we feel deeply purified.

We eat a newly harvested plum and our cells lighten. Dewy parsley brings forth the hero in us. Fresh beets warm our heart. Hiking on quartz clears our mind. Playing on a sandy beach generates flexible attitudes. Planting seeds engenders hope for the future. Climbing a tree expands our considerations. Pruning helps us release the old. Burning windfall begets gratitude for transformation and warmth.

Warren Grossman attributes miraculous curative powers to conscious and physical connection with the living earth. Donna Eden teaches us to align and work with natural healing energies. Rosemary Gladstar shares herbal potions. Traditional Chinese Medicine works with, and through, the physical, to shift body and mind. Derived pharmaceuticals mend both our body and emotions. The list continues.

However you shape your own understanding, and relationship, with the natural world, I encourage you to celebrate the unique experiences. We know the wellspring of joy available. We must each have an individual relationship with primal being. Nature's grace is always at hand.

Healing Our World

At times my heart is heavy. I feel sad about the walls of difference we build and the intolerance we magnify; fear then motivates our actions.

As I gaze into our possible future as a human family, I see that one of the medicines for our time is the habit of increasing our range of perspectives. We then invite new insight and perhaps most importantly, humble ourselves. Do any one of us really have 'the answer'? I think not. The practice of being comfortable with uncertainty is a great beginning. The practice of both sitting low and accepting personal responsibility also opens us to wondrous rarified experiences. We cannot summon the numinous, but we can cultivate the receptive, welcoming attitude that prepares the ground.

While reading this book I call on you to stretch your imagination, suspend assumptions and recover innocence. We know that no one is exactly like me or exactly like you. To be together, really together, we must acknowledge this. We must also know that as well as difference, there is a pervasive underlying connection and, deeper than that, common vitality and essence.

Section 2. Stirring Perception

The stories in this section are told through two lenses. One lens is the writer, the other an animal, plant or another person.

The tales are intended to loosen our habitual viewpoint. This new frame of reference broadens our understanding of what is possible.

Lilacs

I see purple dancing through four petaled miniature blossoms.

This course of color travels through winter's long night.

Returning yearly for a spring opening.

She announces herself with a sweet honeyed scent.

My nostrils tingle as I lean close.

I remember an open window near my childhood bed.

At this time of year lilac accompanied me through night journeys.

My father before me, a child in Holland, was soothed by the same fragrance and beauty.

Now I sit on the ground looking up at a mature lilac tree.

We are about the same age.

Both of us have memories.

Both respond to warmth and to the quickening of early spring energy.

~~~

Warmth on my wood, sap flowing . . . again.

A strong force propelling from deep within my roots.

Buds beginning to leaf.

Slow awakening from cold weather slumber.
~~~

Sun high in the northern sky is my alarm clock.

Now the sound of green makes heart shaped leaves.

Hundreds of four petal flowers birth as purple clusters.

Intoxicating scent; set for early bees to harvest my flowing nectar.

This scent brings a young girl.

She bends to smell my buds.

Her skin brushes me.

I leave a trace of pollen on her cheek.

I have a place inside her heart and mind where one of my eternal seeds lives.

I did this for her father too, a gift given freely to both of them.

They carry me and love me.

I live within them both.

Morning Walk

Each morning a few salmonberry buds emerge as fuchsia colored flowers. Yesterday's flowers morph towards small berries.

Emerald green deepens and folds in. This shrouds the skunk cabbage blossoms within enormous leaves.

Yesterday a spider was to my left. Her web was strung a meter wide between two birches. The web is not here today.

This section of the path is visible only as a lessening of lamb's quarters ground cover.

Each morning my sneakers press through leaves, crushing some, disturbing others. The following morning the lamb's quarters is higher, larger and sturdier.

I recognize this path. If I did not, I might be fooled in direction; perhaps I'd follow the deer trail rather than the nature walk carved for retreat center guests.

Large cedar gives way to birch. Birch gives way to Oregon grape and fern.

As I pass over the final bridge, again I am drawn to squat and pee in the same location I was drawn to yesterday and the two days before. Today there is no physical urge, just the beginning of habit. Squatting, growing shoots tickle my bottom. I notice the sharp razor quality of crabgrass.

The sun is higher today. On the beaver pond lilies float; a bright yellow mirror.

Turning a corner at the top of the small hill, the dog gets up from under the fir tree. She comes over and greets me. Last evening,

I spent time scratching behind her ears, stretching her forehead and talking with her. She is aging and perhaps in failing health. I adjust my stance so that she can sniff my hands and legs easily. I want her to feel safe and to know me.

Continuing full circle to the lodge, a beautiful morning walk. A private walk; or was someone watching me?

~~~

I am the songbird seeking trapped insects from the spider's web.

My wing dips down through sticky strands and tears the web.

Spider will rebuild her birch to birch supermarket web later today.

She spins silk, five times the strength of steel, replacing an entire web in an hour.

The fragrance of gigantic skunk cabbage flowers strengthens each day.

Lamb's quarters abound.

Our nest is in the old moss-covered cedar tree.

Eggs are hatching and my babies are singing; still in the nest another week until flight.

I fly over the lilies, drink from the pond, watch over deer, squirrel, and raccoon.

Today another visitor is walking the trail.

She squats to pee just like that old dog.

I wonder if those two know each other?
~~~

Holding Hands

We held hands from the beginning, wordless peace. Holding hands is better than talking. Words can be awkward, like using a shovel to measure gold; missing the mark, wasteful, clumsy. Holding hands was direct connection, soul to soul, complete, safe, more real than anything else in the world.

We held hands walking, at meals, driving, even at rest. When emotions were painful, hard or complicated, we held hands too. It was a way of connecting directly, lovingly in spite of complexity.

Holding hands for years, we got to know each other inside, that part which is full, soft, rich, and overflowing with gentleness. It is a part within us that language still cannot touch; in the same way, the word 'kitten' could not describe the magnificence of a bundle of purring, playful, light filled fur!

I can still hold hands with Gary. The fingers of my left hand curl over to touch the palm. I feel connected in the same way as when he sat beside me. Off to the left I feel his love, bigger than ever, connecting with me, through me, around me. Still easy to hold your hand, though you have no physical body. Still easy to know the 'big' part of you; the part words cannot express.

For two years I cried every day! Cried and held your hand. Finally I accepted, at least in some way, that I would not see you again in this life.

Not as a memory - but as 'Now'; I can still hold your hand, still listen and connect, still completely know you.

~~~
~~~

My wife.

She and I connected like lightening. It was like a global shift somehow restoring balance. We were dumb for words. We met, touched in a simple greeting, and the world changed.

Over time, in the way of earth, we came together as a couple; still not understanding how to describe a connection and perception bigger than language and thought.

We held hands all the time while I was embodied. Holding hands I knew she loved me. I knew a safe harbor on earth. It was the same for her.

I was still a defender then. Employed to battle for justice. Advocate for hire. Demanding toil under a hot sun.

As the cancer grew, there was nothing to say. We held hands. I wanted to stay embodied, to stay with her, but it wasn't to be. We held hands as I left my body, taking a route up her left arm to her heart.

She continues to hold my hand. At first it was every waking moment. In her sleep she'd come looking for me.

She still holds my hand, sees me, hears me, loves me. I watch her wake each morning, shifting and stretching, leaving my side of the bed intact. I love her.

Morning Coffee

The effect on my body impresses. This ritual stimulant calls my sense of smell first. Before boiling the water, or pressing the grounds, I anticipate the reward. I experience waves of roasted, piercing high pitched scent; a scent calling to be prepared. This herbal nutty first calling, has a purely positive association. Later in the mug, the coffee scent will be different, changed in the swirling and pouring, opened and expanded to fill the entire kitchen.

The coffee I drink is harvested continents away. Handpicked choice beans are gathered, sorted, then placed in sixty kilo jute bags for shipment to Italy. Beans are sorted again, this time with image photography to eliminate unfit beans. The roasted packaged coffee is flown worldwide. This fresh rich power is scientifically screened and protected. Arabica beans arrive in vacuum packed tins, pressurized with inert nitrogen. This is MY coffee, full of flavor, aroma and taste.

Here in the sunroom, looking at the arbutus tree, lavender bush, and emerging snow drop buds; a coffee filled cup warms my hands. My shoulders soften. This is a time to relax. This is a declared break from worldly expectation, or the more demanding task-master within my head. I love this ritual! It is a pause that nurtures. Garden beauty streaming into my eyes, comfort warming my hands, vigor returning. I almost hear the coffee speak.

~~~

The world over, people prepare me into a liquid elixir. I am a tonic, a diversion, an invigorator, a comfort, a reason to pause, embracing present moments.
~~~

My mild stimulant was, and continues to be, a cultural mainstay. I was first transported from the highlands of Ethiopia to become popular in Istanbul, Turkey during the mid 1500's. As a specialty drink, I was established in Venice by 1645. As a fashion, I migrated north from Italy.

Sold first as a tonic and curative, I went through decades languishing in the 'unhealthy drink' aisle. Now I am again healthy to consume. Science tells people their minds perform better twenty minutes after drinking me; lungs open for ease of breath, eyes have sharper vision, mood elevates and, if well timed, digestion improves.

Beyond me and before me are other stimulating remedies. Assam tea, green tea, ginseng, and reishi mushroom tea are India and China's contribution to energizers. Stimulants appear centuries back in Asia and Central Europe. Linked to a civilization thriving from 6,000 BC to 3,000 BC, is the drink soma. Soma is also referred to in Vedic texts as a tonic, made from the dried stems and leaves of the ephedra bush.

Through Andean culture, coca tea is the excitant and a curative for clarity and endurance. Andean mummies had coca leaves buried with them 8,000 years ago. Consumption is woven into the Andean culture as tightly as the wool weave of llama sweaters.

Many varieties of coffee are now grown in Central and South America, through an amazing range of techniques. Some techniques are in line with my natural ways, others are aggressive, chemically heavy aberrations.

Each day as I scan the globe, I see my presence increase. I am glad for the pleasure I bring. For many I am the lightest moments of their day, I am the pause, I am a small way to touch happiness.

Boots

I support, protect, care for and love her.

I am culturally iconic and permanent in a world that encourages transient change.

Enduring is a notion defined through my simplicity: rubber, leather, Gore-Tex, stitch and glue. There is a mastery of detail, industrial quality.

All this is required to create a templar knight in boot. Hiking armor!

My padded support caresses her feet.

Outwardly, I am a defender.

Inwardly, I protect the maiden.

I am always ready to go, love a challenge, and I am happiest when in use!

I am reliable.

I am unlike a sneaker, trainer or other sport shoe, looking for a seasonal fling or summer romance.

Rather, this is a long-term relationship.

We travel together, on familiar ground or on totally new terrain.

~~~
~~~

These are my boots.

They have a 'pride of place' by the kitchen door.

Near the purple hiking jacket, white wool cap, and the colorful headband.

Seeing my boots is like seeing a friend, a good friend.

This is an easy open relationship, historically underpinned with years of walking together.

These boots will support me on any journey.

I feel joy pointing my toes and rotating my ankles to completely encase my feet.

Now I am protected.

I can sprint up a hill or splash in a puddle.

We have an enduring relationship.

Like a true friend.

Templar knight of boots.

Hiking champion.

Hummingbirds In Winter

At night, when I sleep, I shift into torpor; this state is similar to hibernation. My body temperature drops to 6.5% of waking. When I do wake, depending on the day, it takes up to an hour to regain full awareness. The night time energy savings helps me survive temperate winters. Humans are doing research about preserving the body with slow metabolism. I've been doing this forever!

Many of us fly south, thousands of miles. When I was young, I wintered in Panama. I flew with my family. My memory is spectacular, knowing every flower and bush in this garden, and in the gardens, meadows, and forests on the long flight path south. Leaving here in August or September, when plump and heavy, we fly south at 25 to 30 miles per hour. Between February and May we return north.

I no longer fly south. There are enough spiders and grubs for protein, a fountain with fresh water, and an infinite supply of syrup from three red feeders. The garden here has grown. There are late and early blooming flowers. On very cold days the feeders disappear at night then reappear before dawn with fresh syrup. Each year a few more of us stay north. We flourish in a stable environment.

I'm old for my kind, eight years. Few survive beyond four. It was my health that kept me back the first year. As I experienced the ease of a northern winter there was a change. I decided not to migrate. No long flights, drastic weather or birds of prey; owls and hawks were the worst.

I see and hear very well. Before dawn each morning music plays inside the lady's house. Then there is light, more sounds and blinds lift. She sits and watches us drink from the feeder.

She is smiling and relaxed. I've learned that if the red feeder is empty, persistent flying, with piercing focus through the window will bring fresh syrup.

The season has shifted now. Winter is coming. We have a protected perch in the ancient cedar. I will sleep more and more as the days shorten and cool. I will enjoy the clear bright shining sun and will drink and forage easily.

<p style="text-align:center">~~~</p>

Watching the hummingbirds is part of the link, the precious connection with birds, animals, and all of nature. Joy, overflowing really, when I fully embody the feelings. Early in the morning, before first light, I hear them coming. Do I really hear them or is this some adapted sensing that has evolved in me?

I open the blinds. I have a mug of hot lemon water. Hummingbirds are at the feeder. These are precious moments. Quiet inside and out. Time lengthens as I watch. This is the magic of attention.

Most of the tiny hummingbirds have flown south. The feeders last two days rather than a day. Each year the wintering birds have increased, mostly females. Few radiant swatches of male color come to drink.

I feel responsible, recognizing that part of their wellbeing is reliant on fresh water and syrup. Over the years I have adapted. I rotate feeders, attend to temperature forecasts, and enlist friends to help on days I will be away. They have molded, changed, and willingly enlisted me.

The season has shifted. Winter is coming. I watch the ancient cedar knowing there are tiny homes nestled deep within. I will look inward more as the days shorten. I will enjoy the clear bright sun when she shines and continue to take pleasure in all of nature.

St. Mary Lake

Tentative at first; stepping into the lake in early summer, warmed by June's heat, magnified in the afternoon sun. Belly contracts as I encounter cool velvet water touching the skin. Relaxing only after several strokes; belly, bottom, shoulders soften. Legs and arms remember this simple movement. Strength/release, strength/release; advance/accept, advance/accept.

Now September, early morning pilgrimage to immerse 'butt naked' into St. Mary's embrace. Water and body interweave, girl and lake combine. Powerful strokes. Massage of moving water against fingers, toes, arms, and legs. Sun soaked water, rocks, and rice marsh.

Fully supported, abundant; a feeling akin to friendship. Am I anthropomorphizing friendship with the lake or is this true? What does the lake say?

~~~

Someone gave me a name, St. Mary Lake. They did not name the ancient trees who line my sides. There is a girl who comes every year to merge with me. She is nearly 60 now and she is still a girl when we are together.

When the summer leaves begin to turn color in autumn, she then remembers how to talk with me. Her body alternately taut and at ease, can feel my support, feel my nature, feel my history.

This morning I notice her mind release deeper. There is more space for us to relate, merge, know. I feel she is a friend. She can know me as I am, experience me, as I experience her. The
~~~

wild rice at my edge looks on. The shale beneath and around me nods; a timeless moment.

Section 3. Shifting Perspective

For shifts to happen we often endure a time of tension and uncertainty.

The polarity of opposites may exist in a situation or within us. We are wise enough not to seek quick solutions, look for distraction, or to over simplify.

The stories told in this section include pregnant tension. Eventually, when this is held, something is resolved; something new emerges.

I Am Tension

I am the space of the unanswered question.

I am unfulfilled hope and unprocessed grief.

I am contracted muscle, mind and consciousness.

Willful engagement magnifies me.

Unsustainable, yet impossible to reconcile.

This is how I relate to time when force is near.

How then do I dance?

I dance in partnership.

Dancing, the space within my polarity both contracts and expands.

The response is turn, spin, and flow.

Once space, as curiosity is added, I bloom with possibility.

I become a fecund sphere rather than a contracted seed.

Many colors, billions of tones, rainbow from my orbital expanse.

Eventually something new will be formed.

This is a totally new understanding, a discovery, a harmony.

These are the words describing the moment I move from dance back into form.

Some dance easily with me.

Some engage tension with curiosity.

Some are excited when they feel me emerging.

For them I am the beginning of discovery.

I am an invitation to dance.

Accept the invitation to dance.

Balance born of discernment and surrender to inquire; these are the shoes to wear.

Sore shoulders, contracted mind and fixed beliefs all benefit from this partnership, twirling.

Like a centrifuge, elements separate.

Particles of belief and patterns of holding expectations loosen.

The color spectrum is no longer black and white.

There are more colors than eyes can register, both seen and felt.

Eventually particles of discreet understanding are possible.

Compassion emerges.

The next form is created.

This particular dance is complete.

Porcelain Memories, Earthen Bowl

Two years ago I was walking by the central square in Santa Fe, New Mexico. It was a warm June morning. I was in town early for a conference. Three sides of the square were lined with gift, jewelry, and art shops. One of the bright spacious stores called me in.

It was the colors that first attracted me; turquoise blue and magenta. I moved to the earthenware display. As I sorted through the stack of bowls, I paid particular attention to the shape drawing me. From the twenty or so bowls one stood out. The bowl that separated itself had both depth and breadth. There was enough depth in the bowl to contain anything that tended to be liquid and enough breadth in the bowl, a wide enough circumference, to make it easy to accommodate utensils. None of other bowls had this combination in conjunction with almost perfect swirl patterns of color. I was happy to purchase a beautiful handcrafted earthen bowl.

Over the years, if I was alone, I ate regularly from the earthen bowl; breakfast, lunch or dinner - didn't matter. It was also the perfect size for a small serving bowl. I'd use this bowl at a dinner party.

Some small pleasure came each time I looked at the bowl, some joy intrinsic to the combined materials. The elements had all come together when the artist threw this particular work. At least it had come together for me!

A few mornings ago, I washed this bowl in the regular fashion and put it in the rack to dry. I turned my head and torso to the right, in the direction of the kettle. From the left I heard a crash. With a pivot, I saw the beautiful bowl shattered on the floor.

Immediately I felt Gary; or rather knew how much I missed Gary still. Gary was my husband. He died of cancer three years ago. He was great for me! Then one day we turned our heads and he had terminal cancer. It is hard to lose someone you love. It is hard to lose a relationship that has depth, breadth and wonderful color. Bending down I collected the earthen shards from my kitchen floor. I placed them together in a beautiful purple porcelain dish. The dish is on the counter behind the stove, under the kitchen gong. In that location there is a clear line of sight from anywhere in the kitchen.

As I placed the bowl I thought of Gary; he still has been a part of each moment, of each day. He is there in the morning on waking, in the kitchen always, at the table, on the sofa in the evening, and snuggled beside me at night. That earthen bowl of experience is shattered. Can't come back.

As I gathered and placed the bowl remains, I found myself making a commitment to get on a little more with this life. I made a commitment that each time the pains of separation emerged, I would think of Gary, and also think of the conversations we would have in the future. Conversations when I'd left this earthen body and was more easily able to communicate with him on the other side.

Healing and shifting happens in so many small ways. Until that beautiful bowl shattered, I had appreciated it daily and assumed it was always available.

Nothing can replace the unique artistry of my Santa Fe bowl, as nothing can replace Gary. Still there is the magic of other artistry here on earth. So much beauty to be perceived and enjoyed. It would be a shame to miss the colors.

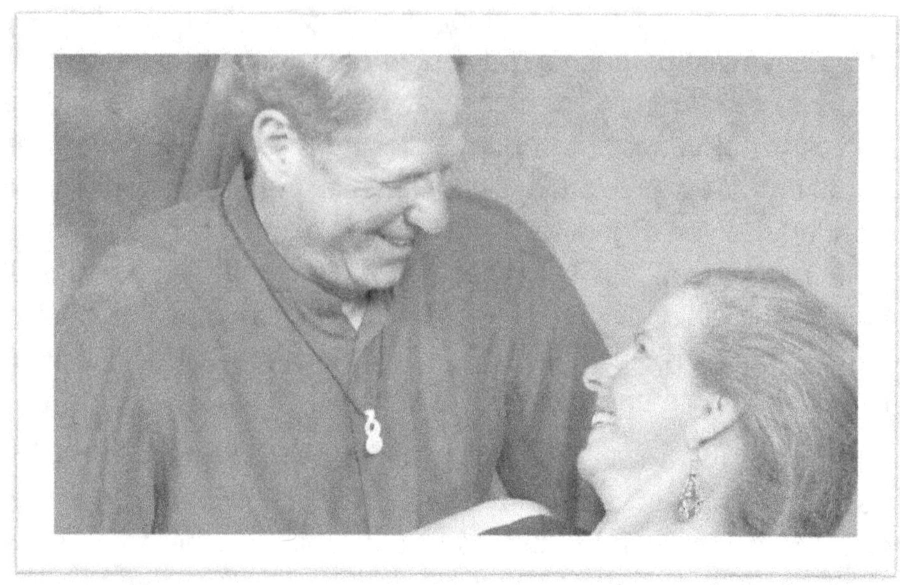

Judgment To Compassion

Here is a friend's story of change; told from her perspective.

Early Wednesday evening I am driving to a friend's house, leaving home a few minutes late. I choose to finish a conversation with my husband rather than leave on time.

As I turn from the side road to the main road, I find myself behind a particularly slow driver. I am frustrated at their slowness, there is driving time to make up to arrive when promised. As our two cars approach the village, my mind envisions the slow driver will pull into the shopping area, getting off the main road. This story fills my head as if it is inevitable! The slow driver does not turn.

Beyond the village, around the corner, and up the hill to the second shopping area, of course they will turn in here. No. Now frustration shifts to judgment and blame. New stories appear in my mind. This driver is the reason I will be late, they are to blame; frustration, judgment, and name-calling.

Past the golf course and still no change in the speed of the driver and no opportunity to pass. Making a left turn at the intersection and heading exactly the same way as me, the saga continues, tension increases. Stress chemicals; adrenaline, cortisol and norepinephrine flood my body.

A few blocks before arriving at my friend's home, my awareness shifts. A new mental image appears, the vision of an elderly driver in front of me, someone timid to be driving at night. I imagine a cautious, light sensitive, elderly person ahead. My heart finally softens.

Shifting from frustration and judgment in my head, shoulders and belly, to a softening at the chest and heart I feel more relaxed. The fault and the blame isn't to be placed on this driver.

If I had truly wanted to be on time, I would have finished my conversation with my husband and left the house with extra minutes to spare. Likewise, being a few minutes late, in this situation, is not a difficulty. Certainly not important enough to flood my body with stress chemicals.

~~~

The chemical benefit to my body, of being in a state of compassion and gratitude, is the polar opposite of the detrimental effects of stress. Once I switch to feeling compassion, the increase in available serotonin supports a healthy body function. I am taking better care of myself by 'cutting the other driver some slack'.

The ten minute drive took me through multiple mental and physical states. Frustration built to judgment and blame, then at some point a pivot happened. I shifted as a new idea came into awareness; giving me perspective. I may never meet the driver of the other car. And it doesn't matter. One thing that's profoundly important, is what was happening chemically within my body. Curiosity and compassion stopped the surge of harmful chemicals. I stopped hurting myself. This lessened the likelihood of disease caused through stress and anxiety. Most of us understand that stress releases a cocktail of chemicals which are hard on our body. Yet in the moment, we still get frustrated with the driver in front of us. We still blame others for things that we could take care of ourselves.
~~~

Forest

Dense, thick, slow, wet. Bright emerald green and jasper; needle and foliage. Bloodstone colored soil. Platinum rock and lichen; white, grey, crystal quartz colors glimmering through. These are forest jewel tones.

Breathing is easy with fresh moist air. My lungs are relaxed. Forest fragrance is light and sweet, almost too weak for my human nose to register. When I listen hard with my nose, I isolate that sensing organ. Other senses diminish. Now I register the subtle and complex scent of the forest. This aroma is alluring. It is inviting me in.

Forest scents come alive after a storm. Fallen trees are broken open. Cedar is dominant; stronger than fir, pine or maple. Cedar shouts in sweet intoxicating herbal notes. This is an alto scent; not soprano, nor tenor, nor bass. Harmonized to refresh and enliven, stimulating the feeling of deep sustainable strength and inner restoration. I breathe in the power of cedar.

As I walk, the ground varies. Soft fir needles and rotting logs. Old brown of decay is the composted mingling of many previous lives. The soil is fertile, ready as a support system for new birth.

How can we perpetually look at the cycle of life in only one quadrant, elevating birth and life above decay and death? What do I lose when I put blinders on my eyes and devalue the cycle as a whole? Did I separate decay as bad, elevate growth as good? What would endless growth be? No time for reflection, release, amends, and reforming. So much insight depends on the failure of the old tree, old idea, old system, old scientific understanding, or old world view. With time the composting cycle is complete, ready to support new seeds.

Here a douglas fir and western red cedar have grown together. Their seeds began apart. Time has increased their girth and height, first the blending of barks, now intermingled. Like couples growing together in relationship.

Arbutus is the wild spirited reggae dancer of this mountain. While other coniferous trees reach directly to the sun, arbutus is chaotic! Beyond jazz or hip hop, this is an ode to unbridled inventive force. There is no ordered growth in the madrone family. There is no linear dominance in her theme. She is the unceasing adolescent among stands of vertical efficiency.

Sword fern, Oregon grape, salal; perpetual color unperturbed by winter's harsh cold or summer's drought. Shade growing, save where cedar has acidified the soil to define her turf. Growing bush abounds. Dense branches are encouragement to stay on my path.

The pileated woodpecker's hammering echoes for miles, pygmy nuthatches flutter. Spotted owls are silent. In spring, turkey vultures and eagles soar. Here eagles are common. They travel through this forest on the way to Alaska. This is a highway stop. Fast food; mouse or rabbit and a night's rest.

Squirrels scamper from sounds or sit motionless waiting for a threat to pass. Today I am the threat. She sits on a broken limb waiting for me to go. I linger, she maintains her stillness. My attention shifts to reach for my camera. She is off, behind the fir, down through leaf covered forest floor.

Deer are silent watchers and silent walkers. Now deer eat the leaves of newly fallen arbutus and maple. A noisy risk defying eagerness prevails, stretching prudent safety limits. These are a favored delicacy. She doesn't notice me until I am very close.

There is no silence in the forest. Listening, tuning in, savoring; the sound expands. Around and through me, not one note, or several, but many blending together. I recognize this sound. In my body I know this is an old and important sound, yet my mind does not understand. What understanding comes, enters through the body; it is the feeling equivalent of translation.

At journey's end I am refreshed, enlivened, vibrant. What combination of elixir was administered? This was scent, sound, moist air, full life cycle emersion; enchantment of the forest experience.

Scape Dog

Listen as another friend shares her story.

It was a hot dry August day on the Gulf Islands. Three generations, two families were sharing a small home; my new husband and I, my daughter, her two children, and a big boisterous dog. One of my grandchildren was very ill. Tensions of uncertainty permeated each of our inner landscapes. None of us could express our deepest fears. Each of us were packing layer upon layer of stress into our imagination. So much pressure. A rupture was inevitable.

Patterns of life had shifted. There was risk and uncertainty. Everything within me wanted stability. The fluctuating experience of those close to me, and real medical challenges, made my life feel very risky. None of us were sleeping well. Lack of sleep magnified lack of clarity and jagged nerves. That August afternoon eighty pounds of canine volatility epitomized the entire challenge.

How could I blame my daughter for her parenting or blame the children? How could I reconcile grandchildren being unwell and in need of specialized medical attention? How could I express all my fears for the future to others when I was afraid to even feel or name them myself?

What I wanted to happen in my life seemed way out of my reach. I was searching for some kind of ground. I wanted to feel in control, to make some part of our family story better. If I could not blame myself or those around me, who could I blame and where could I take back some small sense of power? What change would make things better?

The dog has to go. My scape dog!

Banishing uncontrolled buoyancy would bring order to everything. At least that seemed possible in the moment. In that moment it was easy to imagine that removing Max, the fun seeking dog, would resolve all family challenge.

I had made a decision. As a loving parent I prepared and rehearsed what I considered tactful words. I stepped out of the main house, intent on confronting and solving the obvious problem, Max.

Walking across the parched gravel driveway to where my daughter sat taking shade under a filbert tree, I saw something I hadn't seen for months. My daughter was smiling. She was snuggling the eighty pounds of fur, dust, and activity, the dog. I watched her receive comfort in an easy manner. Her shoulders were soft. Her face relaxed. She smiled, leaning easily into Max. In fact, she was more relaxed and vulnerable than I had seen in years.

As a family we had been so locked in confrontation, crisis management, and problem solving that there had been no easy comfort. All conversations were dominated by attempts to manage the unmanageable. We all tried to be strong.

As I walked through the scorching sun intending to initiate a conversation banishing the dog from the property, everything changed. The solid ground of insistence gave way. Rather than needing to reestablish a silent pet free property, I opened. I began to see that this dog was a life-line, a love-line for my baby girl. My baby girl was now a mother with her own children and with huge responsibilities, yet she needed to be able to let down her guard and play.

My own anxiety over the complex situation meant that our relationship was not an easy one. My daughter could not receive comfort from me. Yet, here she was at ease with that big dirty hound.

I watched her shift from twenty-five years old to five years old. She changed from seemingly belligerent, to a young girl trying to do her best. In that moment I too became a girl trying my very best. In that moment we were not separate; we were all held together in a larger embrace. My pace changed. I entered the shaded area. I shared a few words with my daughter then I returned to the main house.

In the following weeks my husband and I became friends with Max the dog. We learned how to play. We learned it wasn't the dog that was bad, but lack of discipline and structure that brought unwelcome outbursts.

Slowly we created an environment to support the best life for each of us. I moved from trying to control an uncontrollable situation through brute force, to a place of embracing the simple moments we had together. We were humbled. The humility brought us together as individuals doing our very best, facing a challenge beyond our control. The new emotional space we inhabited was soft and caring rather than harsh. We laughed and played a little more. Often this was initiated by Max. Over time, the unsolvable problems shifted. Strategies emerged.

~~~

Fear and uncertainty were magnified when it appeared there was no path for resolution. It is easy to take discomfort and then project the problem on those we love. It is natural in times of tremendous stress to want to control something, anything. We look for something that is safe to diagnose. In this case it was easy to find a 'scape dog'.

I shifted from trying to control the behavior of my daughter and my daughter's adopted stray dog, to the experience of appreciation for the challenges she was facing. The shift brought softness to our relationship and simple appreciation for the demands in each of our lives.
~~~

Infantry Soldier

My father was an infantry man, a child soldier at fifteen.

This is about war. And this is about multi-generational imprinting.

My father fought in World War II. Towards the end of the war, there were only forty men in his unit. In his final battle, all but three were killed. It's a miracle he was saved, that he was even collected from the battle field.

He was shot in that battle. Six bullet wounds penetrated his chest, skull, arms, groin, and one of his legs. I never asked the details of how, while bleeding out, he was removed from the field, imprisoned, and survived afterwards. What I do know I can share with you.

This was near the end of World War II. He was kept alive but that wasn't enough. Most of his skull was destroyed, eventually replaced with a metal plate. His groin was mutilated. There was no sexual function. In time many other wounds healed, leaving scars on his face, arms and legs. The big challenges were sexual function, skull reconstruction, and plastic surgery for his face.

After the war, to raise money for restorative surgery, my father smuggled items between Holland and Germany. One memorable story I heard as a child, recounts smuggling size ten women's shoes. In Germany, the shoes achieved a very high price from a particular fräulein. For several years he smuggled to raise sufficient funds for multiple surgeries. His will to survive, his instinct to live, was remarkable. Other stories include living for days on nothing but discarded coffee grounds and hiding in root cellars.

As a young child, when visiting Holland, my father took me out on cloudy nights, near the time of the new moon. He described how to sneak across borders. You get low, flush with the ground, crawl down the side of the dike, slip slowly through the water, then climb up the other side, always watching for patrol guards.

I visited Holland regularly the second and third decade after the war. At that time the dominant feeling in Europe is expressed in the prevalent saying, 'never again'. So many families were suffering. Everyone was touched. My father's family had spent time in prisons and concentration camps, they had lost valuable items and land. Devastation prevailed. The visceral commitment was to avoid war in the future; at any cost.

Now when I go to Europe, the younger generation does not remember World War II. They have no experience of widespread loss, imprisonment, occupation, physical pain; rather they are buoyant and forward looking. I am happy for this positive perspective.

As a child I lay for hours on my father's chest, delighted to be smiling and laughing, meeting his gaze. This baby-me was close to his heart, feeling his love, yet also absorbing his anguish. He had frequent nightmares throughout life, waking in terror from relived suffering.

The result of laying on my father's chest, loving my father, hearing his stories, naturally resulted in my subconsciously internalizing his feelings surrounding the war. Throughout my life I have had a profound understanding of the suffering associated with battle and occupation. The imprinting caused me to react in a reflexive manner to various other war stories. This is particularly true of stories that presented black and white perspectives of war.

It was only recently that I took the time to 'feel' into my father's lived experience of the final battle; where he was an adolescent wounded with six bullet holes. Some bullets remained lodged in his body, some passed through the flesh, through the muscles, and exited on the other side. In imaginatively reliving his experience, my context of understanding deepened. I could honor my father's memory in a new way. By letting the feeling and body memory become conscious, I felt a form of embedded sorrow that had subconsciously permeated my psyche.

Discussing the war had never shifted my sorrow. Rationalizing failed to free me. Allowing myself, as a strong adult grounded with a sense of identity, to feel into and imagine living this battle, resulted in lifting my sorrow and pain. I have not lost my appreciation for the suffering of war, but I have managed to dissipate the uninvited pain. I no longer need to carry this. The infantry soldier can rest in peace.

This personal story is an example of the work we can do releasing trauma passed on to us from our parents. Many of us have known challenges and suffering. Sometimes we see how, for unexplained reasons, aspects of our parent's story have come forward as habits in our life. We may have tried many techniques to alleviate this particular inheritance, yet still feel dominated by the power.

By reimagining and feeling deeply into the old trauma, loosening its grip, loosening the tentacles woven throughout the strands of DNA, I can now love my father more deeply than ever before. For the rest of my days, I have profound gratitude for the experience of a peaceful life.

Peace Eagle Authority

Here is another's poignant experience.

I listened to the experts, looked at the blood tests and MRIs with my own eyes; educating myself as I conferred with my medical team. Eventually some kind of acceptance happened. There was resolve and the operation was my choice. Not only was it clear that I wanted the procedure, I also felt positive about the outcome.

The day my surgery was scheduled my husband and I left home early. We caught the ferry and were on our way. I sat in the passenger seat as we traveled winding country roads. Emotionally, I kept what can be best described as neutral positivism. This was not my first cancer surgery. I knew some of the twists and turns to expect.

Partway into our journey we noticed the swoop of broad wings, a turkey vulture to our left. In my tradition, turkey vulture is known as the peace eagle. Protection and guardian energy are two of her attributes. Her scientific name, Catharses Aura, means Golden Purifier. She has great vision. She was a welcome visitor on our journey.

I have heard others reflect on the unspoken confidence these vultures have. You rarely hear praise for the skill or gifts of the turkey vulture; never praise for their beauty. Yet, in spite of being unfashionable, these birds carry themselves with grace and ease. Little did I know I would be unfashionable later that day.

The peace eagle stayed with us for several miles. She flew ahead, easy to view from the car window. Before we turned into the hospital, she dipped her wing toward me and then flew north.

I was gowned, 'gurney-ed' and ready for the operation. In the operating room about to receive anesthetic, I said a confident 'no'. I said no, with the inner authority that not one person questioned.

To this day, I don't know where this 'no' came from. Friends have asked if there was kinesthetic knowing or direct insight. I can't answer. All I know is that I said a very unfashionable 'no' to the operation that day, at that hospital. I stood my ground gracefully.

With every fiber of my being, leaving that operating room was the only path. In spite of a disruption to hospital schedules and staff, nothing in me was willing or able to submit to the potentially life-saving operation.

Out of the operating room, I dressed and walked to the waiting area. There I met my very surprised husband.

When I am asked about this disruptive decision it is still hard to describe. The confident 'no' was bigger than the day-to-day me. My average nature is polite and accommodating. That day there was no accommodation. Likewise, there has never been a moment of regret. Nor has there been a need to understand the greater mystery held in that moment in time, that 'no'. I continue to feel a deep rightness with the decision, peace eagle rightness.

Weeks later I had an operation in a different hospital. The surgery was successful and I remain cancer free four years later.

My story has parallels with decisions many of us make, decisions that seem out of sync with the wishes of others or the norms of a group. Trusting the wisdom of my own deep knowing and learning to accept my own authority, continues to be a growing edge. I love the memory of this experience. It supports me on my path.

A Dream That Changed A Marriage

This story of change is told from the dreamer's perspective.

It was a dream that changed my marriage. "Don't turn too soon", that's what the dream said. "Don't leave this country road, this dirt road. Don't leave this committed though uncomfortable path." At first, I didn't hear the dream message. On reflection I listened.

The fullness of the dream depicted all the suffering that we were locked into in conscious life and also held keys. In waking life my partner and I were preparing to end the relationship. We had already separated from each other in many small ways.

In the dream I am traveling a humble dirt road. I am outside the municipal and county roadwork jurisdiction, outside major pathways. The road has muddy potholes and random boulders. It is night, with a cloud covered sky; dark. Almost no light guides me.

Intuitively I know there is going to be a change in direction. There is discomfort, tension in my dream belly. Whatever is coming feels like unknown territory. I know the next turn is a little distance ahead. In my dream, I act too early. In the dream I recognize the wiser turn was further along than I chose. Turning too soon takes me into a fierce encounter.

I park. Big male energy, in the form of several men, gather around me, threatening my being, my identity. I am aware of the threat to my car, my way of being in the world, and the threat to my identity, my pocketbook, my purse. I want out! Emotions are disheveled, disorganized, scary, and incomplete. This is what I am encountering in the dream. In waking life, my intimate relationship is also threatened.

Is the dream simply mirroring the waking discomfort, suggesting a relationship end? No, this is not the story as I reenter the dream. Rather, the dream is showing something else. The dream highlights me at the driver's wheel, in full control, intuitively knowing that I should stay the course and yet exiting the road prematurely. How is this true? The second scene in the dream shows me in fear and confronting issues of identity and issues of big masculine energy. I feel unsafe.

Awake I reflect about roadways. I consider the traditional way our roads are constructed; earth foundation, sub grade, sub base, base, and then the surface. The roadways we travel in life are engineered for speed and ease, so too with most of our social relationships. Surface encounters facilitate achieving many of our goals. They are fast, they are smooth. And what are we resting on?

The metaphor in my dream reminds me of the simple human earthen foundation we are. We all have a few loose boulders and muddy holes. In the dream I have been brought down below the superficial surface of pavement, well below the quarter inch polite asphalt covering, brought down to the dirt and essence of being, the earth. That's where both my partner and I are in waking life. We are also both bitterly sad, unable to express the heartache that overwhelms us.

As I live with this dream and give the benefit of the doubt to the intuitive wisdom in the dream, a dialogue opens. My partner and I talk more. I consider that perhaps I am turning away from yet another relationship too soon; from this profound connection with another soul.

With the humility of a dirt road, clay to clay, we sculpt conversations. These conversations breathe new life into our understanding and appreciation. Both of us are enlivened and invigorated; giving birth to greater knowing of ourselves and the 'other's' being.

We are fashioning the sub grade, sub base, and base of our relationship. This new base supports a surface that can withstand wear. In hot and cold moments, we resist cracking. Emotional weather solicits fewer random muddy dips, or hard obstinate boulder like reactions.

My identity was being threatened in the dream and in waking life. I had to leave behind associations of formative loss. The dreamscape presents strong male energy; instinctual energy wanting to be seen and heard, wanting to have love reciprocated. I too want love reciprocated and yet I had become such an old road, wanting a quick turn to avoid historic disappointment.

This dream teaches me not to turn too soon, not to turn away from something rich and viable with an earthen base. This dream teaches me to get down below the asphalt coverings of polite surface communications. Below the bituminous tar quality of old emotional memories, I learn to feel the humble pathway, the ground of being.

Because I am listening, something new is being built. A worthy foundation is saved. My partner and I meet at a deeper, more vulnerable level than we have ever known. We are firming our relationship through conversations and kindness and we are leveling our basic relatedness through actions. This is saving my relationship and enriching my life.

~~~

Note on dreams

From the perspective of many indigenous and religious traditions dreams are part of our wholeness. Dreams are a part
~~~

of our wisdom. The fullness of my friend's physical and emotional experience during her dream, as well as her dream symbols, precipitated a shift in her perspective. She shifted from needing to feel agency and control during a time where lifelong emotional reactions were being challenged. She shifted towards the simple, humble, ground of being. Close relationships periodically reduce us to the earthen base of our natures. At best, we are able in our nakedness to come face to face with those we love.

Trees

Each morning I meditate; lake ahead, madrone behind, pine to the west, cedar with sun rising behind her to the east. Trees and lake mark the perimeter of this land.

We harvest drinking and irrigation water from the lake. We enjoy fresh oxygen supply from the fifty odd working trees. Like working animals, these trees support human life. Like animals, they have feelings that are invisible to us.

It took time to build communication links with these trees and it took body knowing. The first night I deeply connected with the trees was after I'd hired a faller to remove the central tree line that would open my line of sight to the lake. At 3:00 a.m. a chorus of sorrow swept through my body. The tree's dying screams felt deafening, their pain pervasive, for one week, night and day; then finally reconciliation.

In *The Secret Life of Plants*, Tompkins and Bird argued that danger, threat and pain cause the greatest measurable electrical response from plants. Later the authors detail individual supportive relationships between plants and people. Similar research continues today. Science is measuring plant kingdom intelligence.

Ten years ago, an unconscious action on my part caused great pain and also blessed me with new sensitivity. I've cut trees since then. When I do, I meditate, consult with the great cedar, feel into the trees I want cleared and open a path for their easy transition. Tompkins and Bird compare Kosher slaughter and possum fainting to the way plant vitality disappears when faced with predetermined death.

Cleve Backster's experiments showed that trees remain attuned to each other for hundreds of miles. Similarly, Candice Pert, an internationally recognized pharmacologist, argues in *Molecules of Emotion*, that each cell in the human body is part of our way of knowing. Each cell has intelligence, receptive and communicative capability and agency to act or change.

I feel relationship with these trees and this land regardless of distance. When I travel, and seek support or grounding, I mentally connect with the cedar and pine on my land. Immediately my energy shifts, becomes centered and strong. This reflects how I 'know' the trees. I know them inside me and feel they know me. Where eyes, ears, mouth and hands fail, I still know them. Is this distributed molecules of intelligence; or perhaps some yet unnamed awareness that is synced in relationship?

Each morning I meditate; lake ahead, madrone behind, pine to the west, cedar with sun rising behind her to the east. Trees and lake mark the perimeter of this land. Cedar and pine hold me. The land I share with earth, stone, tree, plant, deer, rabbit, and bird; our home.

I Know You By Heart

Dear friend, I know you by heart.

I know you in my poetic mind.

I understand you through a felt sense.

I feel you.

To understand myself and to understand you, I am directed towards my heart.

I am directed by my indwelling soul, my psyche, the loving part of my being.

Modern left-brain communication fails.

Intellectual discourse is incomplete.

Dear friend I know you by heart.

I do not understand all of your inner landscape. Much of you is a mystery to me.

I recognize and respect your 'otherness'.

I accept mysterious spaces.

I include curiosity. My friendship is innocent.

You are bigger than I understand.

There is no expectation.

Chest softens, hard places relax and I feel you with a physical sense. Time stops.

I can let complexity stand even when this makes us uncomfortable.

I can avoid 'pat answers' that would abbreviate your essence.

I can listen and inquire, honoring your emergent nature.

I can let you have space to blossom, contract, change, express.

~~~

We naturally seek out the open hearted knowing with resonant 'others'; be they our particular beloveds, children, friends, or pets.

This is a different way of relating than is commonly practiced.

We all seek heart knowing.

Regardless of rational thinking and modern psychology, we humans have not migrated away from placing the greatest weight on body knowing and heart knowing.

~~~

In The Dark I See A Vision

In the dark, I see a vision.
Eyes closed to facts and time.
Forgetting past and its assumptions.
Ideas birth.

I sense a way of feeling forward.
Wondering, what wants to come.
A flower's potential, latent yearning,
Seeds active.

Imagination, that's the highway.
Open gates, where boundaries held.
Stretching beyond existing knowing.
Surprises welcome.

Dark times invite potential.
Light so bright the sun might cringe.
Trusting into possibilities.
Grounded, daring.

Solitude

Come to me.

Do not fear me.

Step out of the marketplace of time.

Return to a home you have always known.

Do not be distracted by the dragon jaws that seem to adorn my entryway.

The dragons, serpents, and dark creatures are illusionary images created by the part of you that thinks it is not beautiful.

I know you are beautiful.

Come to me.

Let the clothing of this lifetime slip from your shoulders.

Sit with me as a lover touching the solitary strength of my essence.

At once material and immaterial we merge.

Come to me.

Let me be your secret pleasure, your untold rendezvous.

Keep me covered. It serves no end to share our stories.

How can the magnificent be reduced to words?

Come to me.

Section 4. Numinous Moments

I titled this section numinous moments to avoid terms that have become the jurisdiction of particular philosophies, religions or systems.

For centuries we have heard tales of the extraordinary. Some of these tales have shifted the course of our collective understanding, others are highly personal, still others have been denied, buried and forgotten.

We cannot demand the transcendent. We can be open, then cultivate and welcome moments that appear.

The essence of the stories in this section were shared by several people. In many cases this was the first time they had shared these with another.

I hope these stories encourage you to value your own awe-inspiring encounters.

Invitation To Presence

Presence said . . .

What takes you away from me?

Seduced by thoughts, enticed by distraction.

Do you think you'll feel better if you immerse yourself in your problems?

Or in the stories of another?

You step out of your body.

You abandon this home, this house of the soul.

Some affair of mind takes you to another realm.

It's hard to find you once you have left me.

I wait.

Sometimes, as I wait your lack of attention causes decay.

I am untended.

Your memory of my inner road disappears as you visit the land of thought, distraction, and worry.

What takes you away from me today?

Which story has you running from our shared journey?

What magic door 'complex' did you slip through?

Where have you gone?

I am your earthly home; not merely a body of convenience.

I am the felt being.

I am the vehicle of power.

Through me you cultivate new depth.

With presence, awareness increases, becomes more potent and has more power.

Don't abandon me.

Don't leave me by the side of the road. I will be kicked to the ditch while you engage fancy.

Then when you want me you will have forgotten where you left me.

Please bring me along.

Please inhabit me.

From inside of me you grow, create, and thrive.

I am what you seek, already present.

Color Said, Come Play With Me

Color speaks on her own behalf. The section after is drawn from an artist friend.

Come play with me.

Squeeze me from this metal tube, scoop me from this tub.

Put me on a clean glass palette, engage me.

Use a knife, a brush or your hands and fingers.

Stored energy and expression. That's what I am.

Locked in this case I am pure potential.

I am pure possibility.

Willing to be released.

The moment of opening, air comes in contact with my surface, intention connects with my mass.

The artist places me on a palette.

A new relationship forms.

This is a beginning.

Pure pigment is my essence.

Binder is my skeleton.

Solvent is my connective tissue.

Metal salts reflect the wavelength of color seen, and they absorb all other rays in the spectrum.

Alone in my tube, or tub, I communicate little.

It takes a twisting of the top, the sealed cap, to open possibility.

It takes a desire to release me.

This is a magical beginning.

On the palette, I am joined by other color vibrations.

The selection of colors appealing to my artist this day.

As I look around, I surmise the emotion.

The chosen colors allow me to understand the mood we will be exploring.

Will I represent a sentence or paragraph of the visual dialogue?

Will I be an accent, a comic burst, or a note inserted to magnify the presence of others?

Am I to be a singular expression of something that was, is, or is yet to come?

Beginnings.

Alternate paths, alternate possibilities abound.

A physicist would call beginnings, my state on the palette before the painting process, as a wave form, and I remain thus throughout much of the artistic process.

There is suggestion, there is change, there is painting, scraping and repainting.

A dynamic dance occurs as the elements of color and artist combine.

Each emotional and chemical reaction is unique.

From a point of origin, the new emerges.

Alchemy, we change.

~~~

And the artist said . . .

Joy mixed with wonder and appreciation, this is my feeling while gazing into a tub of paint.

The intensity, the depth and purity of color is rich.

It is akin to seeing a ruby sunset, hummingbird or the ocean.

Magenta, cobalt, teal and cadmium red are obvious beauties; dioxazine violet has hidden complexities.

New tubs tightly closed. I unscrew the lid of the first color.

Scooping a wet silky mass of glistening color onto the palette is visceral.

Part of my choice is conscious; I have an idea of what wants to be created.

A larger part of my process is below the surface, colors 'pop me' and attract my eye.
~~~

I assemble the participants in this afternoon's dance, composition, or song.

The canvas is prepared. I begin. Rather, the soft spot within my belly begins.

There is little thought of a final image.

Thought was surrendered during preparation.

Blending an abundance of paint frees my creative spirit.

I invite the accidental.

I combine knowledge, spontaneity, and happenstance.

Now there is unrestricted joy.

I am the beauty of blending colors.

I experience new color combinations, new color sentences, new inner expression.

I paint a vision.

Conscious mind meets subconscious mind; focused creativity.

We have all been to this connected location.

It can seem like a hard place to get to.

This inner state is self-fulfilling, abundant flow.

I use the term spontaneous expression, yet I know this term is surface to the depth of my experience.

I paint with a waterfall flowing through me.

I communicate some of the flow as expression in today's painting.

Others will look at the work and comment on the skill, nuance, and grace.

For me the greatest gift is the creative flow which fills me, then rushes on.

I admit the reason I bow at the altar of creative expression is ultimately selfish.

I know I drink from this water and stand in this outpouring, for the ecstasy of wholeness.

Ultimately this dance with color is selfish work.

Ultimately it is the alchemy I desire.

Ecstasy's Doorway

Another's story

The first time I touched him, I loved him and he loved me. Our stories were irrelevant. Pure awareness transcended the tug of 'us'. It was true for us from the very beginning.

When we merge physically and in love making, we are together with something essential in the other and in ourselves. The feeling is more ancient than sex, more ancient than opposites coupling. This paths back to complete interconnections. Dare I say cosmic.

We were not young lovers. We had loved, had lovers, been married, had great sex. Our story is of a different ilk. This is a syncing, and an alignment that in a way is completed by, rather than culminating in, endorphin infused orgasm.

We had been friendly for several years, not physical friends, socially friendly. We partly knew each other. We knew a bit about the stories of each other's life and our worldly preferences. We didn't know each other until we touched each other and then the recognition was immediate; then we knew each other before the bone.

Early on we tried to talk on the phone, it was frustrating. When we touched each other there was an eternal connection. From the time we first made love, we knew we were going to be together.

This was not a logical partnering. I was engaged to someone else, ready to leave the city. I had two young children. He was sixteen years older, had children and did not want to be in another parenting relationship. Yet when we touched, the entanglement of our storied lives unraveled. Unraveled to a clear path. Structured thoughts disintegrated. The worlds that separated dissolved. What remained merged.

The physical connection between us is a spiritual practice. Together in communion, not even penetrative communion, visions abound. Visions give way to non-dual, non-local awareness. Whose body is this? Whose hand, arm, leg? What blue mandala song is dancing this exchange? Is this the beginning of time or the timeless? I am I, I am thou, I am not. Both strong and yielding, undone yet safely contained.

Suburban Asheville or forest meadow, we join outside of our own boundaries. By grace we connect, release, plummet, soar and spiral. By grace, ego identity thoughts melt away, a location that is open and full, weaving and simultaneously clear, landscapes itself within us. This is the connection you would go to the meditation cushion for, or the psychedelic opening you would take mushrooms for; this is an embodiment of the 'pure', then 'united' awareness.

Tuned by magic. Vowing not to awake without the other. We go into the place where neither you nor I exist, where all of you and all of I exist.

Learning to release more and more into this space, for me, healed painful attachment dramas. Whenever I'd get scared and want to run away, all we had to do was touch to reaffirm our honest deep love. Hearts beating together, regulated. Hand to hand, chest to chest.

The essential story of our union is a connection with everything in the universe. Our union continues to be the foundation of an extraordinary living practice. Though initially focused on the two of us coupling, the confidence we gained pathed us toward nonegocentric, nonverbal, nonintellectual experience. Love.

After twenty years, we continue to commune physically. I can also more easily connect with the work that I do, aware of the interconnected presence with other people. What has blossomed, are skills to shift beyond and before the ego structure of separateness. In this way I connect with clients in the therapy work I do, with our families, with nature in the woods, beach, and mountains, and with community.

Ocean wave. Salt water.

Sandpiper in me.

Ion rich wind woven through form.

Long view. Another continent connects with attention.

Light beams travel an unseen structure.

Contained and open.

Love holds this consciousness.

No physical form.

Safe to disband what I thought was me.

Now we are both non-dual meditators. We did not know these proclivities in ourselves but the experience with each other led us down this path.

Can I go to this non-dual location at will? I wish I could. I'd love to be able to exist in this state all the time. I understand others can. That is not my business, not my concern.

I am more and more able to open the door to a non-dual location. There is a body awareness, a body memory I can push into. I know where to place my attention.

The brain does not go away just because the personal story goes away. The problem-solving function of the brain remains. The fiction of who we are and who we are not disappears.

Our union was an invitation to an extraordinary living practice. Our physical union continues to bring us to new points. Our practice is born of no spiritual tradition, nor of language. This is the direct experience of awareness.

I don't know where this is going. What have I learned? What do I know in my body and soul? I know how to return home, trusting the safety of this release.

I shy away from the religious, I shy away from the spiritual, from all the intellectual monikers. I did not come from a religious upbringing. I have no story about what happens at death. I do have direct experience of union, awe, love. I am learning to navigate conscious seas.

~~~

Connecting with cosmic energy, religious or spiritual experiences, can be pivotal. Cherished inner experiences give us the confidence to trust in the soul's impelling, trust the direction our life wants to go. Direct knowing gives us ground to stand on. This story tells one pathway to expanded states, safely navigated, inhabited, and claimed. When our awareness expands into new territories, there is a cultivation period where we explore and gain confidence in the viability. Ego attachment tends to be a slow process. Learning to trust 'surviving and thriving' in a location before 'me and mine' takes strength and practice. Strong love.
~~~

Light Tapestry

This pivotal experience comes from a friend.

It was forty years ago. I can't really explain how my perception changed that day. I can't explain what triggered the shift. Yet this completely changed my perspective. It continues to inform my understanding of relationship and reality.

It's early morning, I am alone in my car driving north on the Don Valley Parkway. In this direction the traffic is light. The majority of drivers are heading south, probably to work in the city. I'm working too, delivering product to one of our customers.

There is nothing unusual about the day; springtime, a few green shoots and buds starting, with a slightly overcast sky. There is nothing unusual about my morning. This is a regular Tuesday delivery. I've been taking this early morning trip north for some time.

In a second, my perception shifts. My eyes register all that is around me as streams of energy. Ahead of me the traffic appears as cars and trucks and also as streams of translucent colored light. Through me, to the side of the car, when I glance to the left or right, the grass and trees are luminous. Rays of color shimmer through and around trees and foliage. The air itself appears as stratified flow of viscous color. The shape and color of light varies slightly between forms. My perception registers drivers, passengers, pavement, trees, as individual entities and as complex light forms. My eyes and body are fully open, or so it seems, taking in formerly imperceivable connections and detail.

Beyond the light, I recognize a kind of warp and weft tapestry of woven energy, connecting all that I see and experience. This warp and weft weaves through me and my car. In this moment I physically understand some new aspect of form. No language is capable of expressing the understanding, but the lesson is there.

How long does my light ribbon experience last? Seconds? Minutes? It is impossible to measure. Do I travel one kilometer or several?

How long does this experience remain vital? This question is easy to answer. During and after this opening, I understand viscerally that we are connected, beyond our limited bodies, through this tapestry.

Over the years, it is not so much that I reflect, but rather that I revisit this vast moment again and again. There is a location in me where the light ribbon luminous highway resides. I remember, feel, and then in some small way also open to understanding that these bigger connections are always present. I remember and am humbled. I remember and I soften. I remember and am aware of the energy I contribute to our collective energy tapestry.

~~~

The experience informed an understanding of the expansiveness and intelligence of life emanating from all forms; and of our mutual interconnection. It was fortunate to have such an experience. It is also wise to accept and nurture the gift of greater understanding. Seers from many traditions speak about our energy connection; they describe nuanced structures. Many of us can kinesthetically feel, or visually see, energy flow. Many of us know the wisdom of maintaining our own clarity, not just for ourselves, but also for the energetic benefit of others. In this story there is the visual and felt experience of woven energy connection, with the visible and with the apparently invisible.
~~~

Healing Lessons

Listen to a healer's story . . .

I'd been a healer for many years, trained in several modalities. I brought relief to my clients both in the short term with symptoms and often in long term with remission. Eventually, over a period of years, there were three new lessons to be learned. I don't know what people would describe these as, but I'll tell the tale as best I can and you decide.

My first lesson came in a semi-lucid dream. The dream setting is an entirely different type of civilization and an entirely different operating theater. The location seemed either far future or ancient past; with a quality of energy that is precise, pristine, and luminescent. As the dreamer, I understand that the knowledge of the healers is greater than that of our current time.

A patient is laying on the table. Healers are using wands of light to work directly inside the patient's body. That is, their hands and wands slip easily through the patient's form and move healing light in figure eight patterns at the patient's chakra centers. In the dream, I am one of the healers, working on the root chakra of a patient. It is natural and easy. Knowingly moving the light wand with my hand, I bring healing and balance. Movement of the light impacts the area and affects the ascending chakras. I am satisfied with the work.

I wake from this dream wondering what the message is. Is this a vision of the future, an alternate reality, or a suggested visualization? Within a few weeks I am told of an ancient Egyptian healing tradition, working with light and paired-crystals.

A few years later there was another lesson to learn, it came in the form of a vision or visitation.

It was summer in the high desert of New Mexico. I completed a fourteen-day physical and emotional cleanse through a modified fast with both gentle and vigorous exercise. My whole being was very light. Meditation was easy. Perhaps this was the prerequisite for the visitation.

One afternoon, after completing several tasks, I lay in the shade to rest. Suddenly I was also in a different time. I could feel my body here on the modern earth, on the hard-packed clay and I also felt myself standing on a dirt road in an ancient time. We wore simple rough clothing. The sun said mid-afternoon. The setting was a similar scruffy desert like New Mexico, yet I knew we were far away. In this parallel experience there were only three of us; a teacher, a patient and me.

The teacher was someone I seemed to know very well, forever; I could feel the center of their being and feel their pristine power and compassion. I had a kind of reverence towards them, a reverence related to pureness and mastery.

On the dirt road in another desert environment I was receiving an important lesson. I was receiving a lesson on healing from someone who was my teacher. The lesson clearly described how to support, by filling another with healing light. The intrinsic healing properties would elevate the patient in whatever way was necessary physically and emotionally.

This lesson went on to describe how long-term wellness depended on the other's ability to maintain the light. Holding the light is how the patient stays well. The lesson informed me that each of us has a responsibility to hold ourselves full of light. This benefits us and is part of the support we share when we are helping another.

Filling another with light, see their highest health, this in itself has healing power, and to the degree that they can continue to accommodate light they will stay healed. This was the lesson.

A third lesson emerged during a client session. I had often felt healing presences in the treatment room. On this day that perception shifted further.

While I held points of the client's body and noticed the energetic and physical shift there was also another image. The second image was a holographic overlay. A snow blue operating room with several healers. These healers were working independently of me. It was as if my work, though useful, also served to hold the client's energetic attention and stability, while deeper more complex healing took place. Since that day, the holographic image continues to appear during many sessions.

These lessons have stayed with me over the years, they inform my craft. I still utilize the various techniques I've studied, I also work with light; both for maintaining my own health and in supporting the health of those around me - family, friends, and clients.

Why Dance?

When I dance, I reach a location that is totally satisfied, complete and alive.

Embodying the universe and remembering, this is the gift.

In the heart of dance there is rest.

I may be physically exerting a great deal of energy, yet in the center, is profound stillness.

To dance this way, you must listen.

If there is music you listen to the music, yet this is not the listening I mean.

Music holds a string for attention of the mind.

Where you attend is deep inside, you are not so much listening as finding continual retuning to dance, interconnected with both form and formless.

People watch me dance and say this is beautiful.

They say what grace, what nuance, what magic.

I know their mirror neurons are responding to something grander.

They are responding to what is shining through, independent of the dancer.

The art of dance is alignment.

When alignment is held, you experience deep energetic caresses, ecstatic celebration, fragments of infinite merging.

Dance moves us.

In these moments dance feels like a constant cosmic wave form, ever present before our thought, expressed through focused attention and skill.

The altar many of us bow at is dance.

Others have prayer, scripture, shamanism, therapy, capitalism, science; the list goes on.

We have dance.

To dance well, we experience the divine.

Dance.

Be curious about inclinations arising.

Explore consciousness from inside of movement.

Nothing is separate, notice what is revealed.

There will be times of slow blending.

Times of profound release.

Unwanteds that hang around just beyond the periphery of sight will surface and vanish.

Tension, anger, sorrow, and regret can hide in the shadows until expression is invited.

In other moments, what is new emerges.

We make sense of the world.

Bright energy leads and restores us.

At heart there is peace.

~~~

And Dance said . . .

Come, get to know yourselves beyond words.

Inquire, be curious souls.

Find my elixir.

Emerge in your own dance.

Your body is not separate from the divine.

Liberate yourself from time.

Transcend, reinvent, transmute.

Remember.
~~~

About The Numinous

Sometimes we get in touch, really in touch with the preciousness of this human life. It can happen in a moment. It can happen when we are in an ecstatic state, struggling for our life, holding a newborn, or connecting with a loved one who has passed.

In this private place the mind comes to a point of confusion, the heart to a place of gratitude, and an absolute wonder permeates the wholeness of our being. Moments like this are a direct experience of a 'reality' that is grander and bigger than our daily struggle.

Over a lifetime, many of us shift from feeling alone and suffering to a completely different felt experience, one of feeling strength, connection, and completeness. In the 'felt place of completeness' we connect deeply with energies that I describe as 'prior to our ego'. We develop the capacity to relax our habitual thoughts and feelings and then open. In solitude, we open the door for numinous immersion.

Profound change can seem to take time. The cards that I, and many of us were dealt, included challenges. Part of the challenge was born of feeling that my problems were unique; that there was no one in my community to help with these particular difficulties, no one who could truly understand them. Most of us have experienced similar feelings.

It is relatively common for young people, in their teens and twenties, to spontaneously experience non-local consciousness and other rarefied experiences. Grace begets a conscious shift; whether for a few moments, hours or a few weeks. Occasions of gentle grace or the eruption of expanded consciousness often leave us looking externally to replicate and integrate these insights.

We may spend weeks and ultimately years integrating. A reliable pathway to the numinous requires attention and habit formation. Our western culture neither validates nor assists us. Some find maps in mystical traditions. Others seek a less ornamental explanation.

Direct experience can be full of love and meaning, yet without skillful integration we may still feel alone. Develop habits to engineer a path. Generate a predictable way to access a greater sense of peace, joy, unity, and wisdom. The pathway is not the numinous; rather it facilitates experience of the extraordinary, the awe inspiring.

This light filled, grace infused state, is always present. The radiant palpitating vitality of creative light is omnipresent. Much of our time, our consciousness is just not able to access this 'location' or experience it.

Greater awareness brings agency and responsibility back to each of us; to our choices every moment of every day. Our feeling of personal accountability increases. What we do matters. All the simple daily choices we undertake matter. Knowing this, imbues each moment with greater meaning, purpose, and fulfillment.

Purpose and meaning are woven together in the individual fibers of our daily activity. It is noteworthy that the feeling of responsibility, and its close friend accountability, increases the feeling of self-authority. This is akin to the feeling of purpose.

So what use is this big bright numinous space? Here mysterious restoration floods our body and mind. We are released of attachments to thought, even attachment to our human story and identity. The overwhelming experience is one of healing and peace. It takes a certain daring to cultivate remembrance of the numinous we know, and to establish habits that support the growth of this awareness. Be daring.

Section 5. Afterword

Colleagues and initial readers of this book requested an Afterword.

They asked me to describe the practice of *active imagination,* give a word on *insight or direct knowing and* suggest how the *Inspired Conversations* card deck is a delightful and poignant means toward shifting perspective.

Active Imagination

Several of the stories in this book utilize *active imagination* as a tool to stretch into the inner experience of nature and inanimate objects. These stories are examples of shifts that individuals experienced, that changed or broadened their perspectives.

Active imagination has long been used as a 'soul tool', expanding our considerations towards meaning and depth. In the west, Carl Jung popularized active imagination as a means of exploring unconscious material and soulful material. Throughout history philosophic and spiritual traditions have made use of this tool. Our scientific inquiry follows a similar pattern. Stretching our imagination is how we grow.

I invite you to take *active imagination* further than you may ever have done in the past. When I work with people in groups and individually, we practice embodying alternate perspectives.

For example we practice:

- Seeing the world through the eyes of another, perhaps even someone from the distant past or far future,

- Looking into the future to divine where a trend is leading,

- Feeling what it is to live in the physical body of another, how they would feel in their feet, legs, hips, shoulders, neck, and skull,

- Imagining what is most important for another person, organization, or country, right now,

- Considering how others understand language and perceive what is said,

- Considering what others fear and desire,

- Reflecting on what these perspectives have to teach us.

Engaging *active imagination*, we escape from our own biased tendencies. Consciously asking questions, we gather profoundly valuable information and may get a more accurate read on a current situation. When engaging in *active imagination*, have a set of questions you cycle through to glean perspective. Also, let your imagination and imaginative conversations shift in the direction intuition or whimsy leads you. You may be pleasantly surprised.

Insight

Insight or *direct knowing* may come as a result of *active imagination* explorations. *Insight* may also simply 'land' in our awareness. In the story *Scape Dog*, my friend has a pivotal moment of insight. In that moment, she understands the scene before her in a totally different way than she did just moments before. Questions like the ones listed here, and the ones in the *Inspired Conversations* card set, can lead to moments of insight. Questions help to preserve flexibility, with a bias to understanding more, rather than a bias toward defending our current beliefs.

Inspired Conversation Cards

One winter morning I woke filled with inspiration. I saw an image for the initial design for what has become this set of conversation cards. That morning I rose, moved to the office and began creating. By mid-day I had a set of fifty prompts. I chose an image for the back of the cards. By evening I had a prototype; a set of cards to explore.

We were near the winter holidays, a time of many friend and family gatherings. In the evenings, after dinner, I brought out the conversation prompts. As small groups, we explored ways to work with the prompts. Three years of testing with friends from all walks of life helped me refine the prompts. There were countless delightful and rich exchanges.

Today this Deck is a blend of light-hearted curiosity and meaningful engagement. As I have tested the cards I have come to know and understand friends and family more deeply. I wish the same for you.

Enjoy the journey.

Donna Eden's endorsement says it all:

"Cornelia Krikke has created simple, yet important and magical cards that have the power to open worlds inside each of us. In our speeded lives, these cards slow us down and yet move us quickly into intimate conversations that create trust in our relationships. They remind us how much more there is inside us and asks the questions that draw us closer to family and friends. I love these cards and highly recommend them."

Finally, Play

If we can play into inquiry and into imagination, we are likely to find gems. Play has soft edges that expand to include, rather than exclude. Play has energy for this moment, the place where everything that ever happens, happens. Play is creative and generative; actively integrating transcendent experiences.

Paint mandalas, write, establish ritual, change actions based on the wisdom inherent in your numinous experiences. Elevate and exalt your own moments of grace. There is no particular need to share these with others. It takes a special person to hold a strong mirror supporting our numinous moments. You may or may not have those people in your life. What you can do is celebrate, bow at the inner alter, dance in the music that flows from within, scribble in partnership with your muse.

Absorb the stories and insights in this book. Share your stories. Share your stories with each other. Share your stories with me; stories@transformative-practices.com.

About The Author

Cornelia Krikke holds an MBA and an MA. She worked for 25 years in Canada's corporate center. As a manager, director, consultant, and academic leader she led change initiatives, developed new businesses, and consulted with many leading organizations. With this foundation she chose to broaden her focus.

A passion for life coupled with a sense of calling to another type of fulfillment, compelled her to deepen training internationally. This led to intensive exploration and mastery in multiple personal development and health modalities and an MA in Transpersonal Studies.

Her business, transpersonal, and creative foundations, provide her with accessible experiential tools that allow her to be a highly effective consultant and coach. As a practitioner, Cornelia works with individuals and businesses facilitating and teaching; life/business planning, individual coaching, EEM, dream work and specialized retreats.

Cornelia is an active sculptor and artist, participating in shows within North America. She is committed to the power and viability of conscious creative action as a means to transformation, health and joy.